Lexile: 1080	Guided Reading Level:
LSU ☑yes	
SJB ☐yes	
BL: 6.7	
Pts: .5	P

THE LIBRARY OF CONGRESS

A TRUE BOOK

by

Allan Fowler

Children's Press®
A Division of Grolier Publishing

New York London Hong Kong Sydney
Danbury, Connecticut

Reading Consultant
Linda Cornwell
Learning Resource Consultant
Indiana Department of
Education

The Thomas Jefferson
Building is part of the
Library of Congress.

Library of Congress Cataloging-in-Publication Data

The Library of Congress / by Allan Fowler.
    p.   cm.   —   (A true book)
Includes index.
    Summary: A brief history of the Library of Congress describing its role
in disseminating information and in collecting, cataloging, and preserving
books and other related materials.
    ISBN 0-516-20137-9 (lib.bdg.)   ISBN 0-516-26107-X (pbk.)
    1. Library of Congress—Juvenile literature. 2. National libraries—
Washington, (D.C.)—Juvenile literature. [1. Library of Congress.
2. Libraries.] I. Title II. Series.
Z733.U6F69   1996
027.573—dc20   96-13871
                                                                    CIP
                                                                    AC

Contents

No matter what your interest—from sailing to cooking to ballet—libraries have books you will enjoy.

A Library for Congress

If you want to read a book about sailing ships or microchips, cowboys or cooking, ballet or basketball—you simply go to the library. Your school library or public library has a book on just about every subject.

But about two hundred years ago, when the United States was still a very young country, there were few libraries. Most Americans lived far away from the nearest library. Among those who had the greatest need for a library were the members of Congress, who lived in Washington, D.C.

To help them make wise laws, senators and representatives needed all kinds of

In the early 1800s, Washington, D.C., was a young city with no public libraries.

Wealthy men, like Thomas Jefferson (left), had libraries in their homes. Monticello, where Thomas Jefferson lived (below).

information. They had to read books on history, geography, science, economics, and law. But in 1800, Washington, D.C., was a rough village, taking shape along the muddy banks of the Potomac River. There were no libraries in Washington. The nearest libraries of any size were in the homes of wealthy men such as Thomas Jefferson.

So Congress passed a bill that authorized using $5,000

Congress in the early 1800s (above)
President John Adams (right)

for buying books. President
John Adams signed the bill
into law. The collection began
with 152 books shipped from
England in 1801.

The Library's Beginnings

The Library of Congress was first located right in the Capitol. When British troops burned the Capitol during the War of 1812, most of the library's books were destroyed. So Congress purchased Thomas Jefferson's personal library. With more than 6,000 books added from

The British burned Washington, D.C., during the War of 1812.

the former president's collection, the Library of Congress became larger than ever. In 1851, an accidental fire burned about two-thirds of the library's books, but they were soon replaced.

Ainsworth Rand Spofford, who was appointed librarian of Congress by President Abraham Lincoln in 1864, opened the library to the general public. Until then, only members of Congress and other government leaders had been allowed to use it. The library acquired so much new material under Spofford's leadership that books filled every available space. Clearly,

The shelves of the Library of Congress overflowed with books (left) while the Thomas Jefferson Building was built (above).

the Library of Congress needed a home of its own.

The Library of Congress moved into its home—what is now called the Thomas Jefferson Building—in 1897. But as the years passed, the library's millions of books outgrew the building. So the John Adams Building was added in 1939. In

1980, the James Madison Building, the largest of the three, was built. Today, the Library of Congress occupies these three buildings on Capitol Hill, near the Capitol itself.

Pictured here are: the Thomas Jefferson Building (left), the John Adams Building (right), and the James Madison Building (below).

Serving the Nation

The story of the Library of Congress isn't just about buildings and books. The library pioneered important changes in the way all public libraries in the United States serve their readers. And the Library of Congress serves the country in many ways.

John Russell Young was the first librarian of Congress after the Thomas Jefferson Building opened. He made it the library's policy to hire women and African-Americans at a time when many employers didn't want to hire them.

The Copyright Office, a part of the library, protects the rights of people who create or publish books, newspapers, magazines,

A staff member at the Library of Congress sorts through new books sent in for copyright.

music, motion pictures, plays, and graphic art. Two copies of every new work are sent in for copyright, and then no one may reproduce the work without the copyright owner's permission.

Before libraries used computer databases, index cards were used to keep track of all library books. This method was developed by the Library of Congress, which prepared cards for each new book it

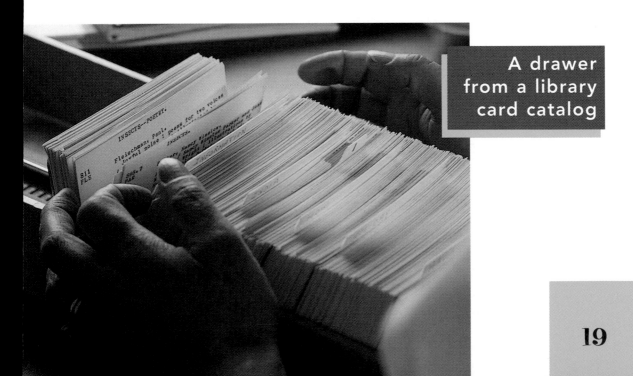

A drawer from a library card catalog

received and made the cards
available to libraries through-
out the nation.

Herbert Putnam, the
librarian of Congress for forty
years beginning in 1899,
helped to create a new way
of organizing books. Your
school library or local public
library may still use the
Dewey Decimal System, but
almost all large libraries now
use the Library of Congress
classification system that

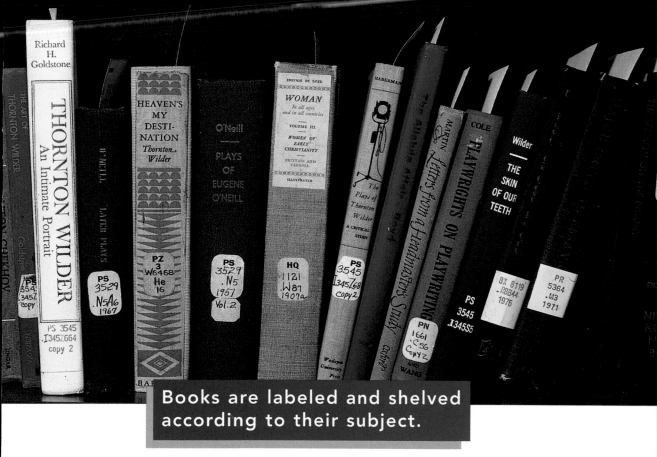

Books are labeled and shelved according to their subject.

Putnam began. A combination of letters and numbers appears on each book's catalog card and on the spine of the book. This method tells you exactly where the book is on the library shelves, along with other books on the same subject. (Look at the page of this book opposite the Table of Contents. It has the same information that appears in the book's catalog listing, including the Library of Congress number, Z733.U6F69.)

During Herbert Putnam's term as librarian, the Library of Congress expanded its services to other libraries, to scholars, and to the general public. But its original purpose—meeting the needs of Congress—was not forgotten. A special division, the Legislative Reference Service, was established in 1915. Later, in 1970, this division was renamed the Congressional Research Service (CRS). Today it has a staff of 860 people. Members of Congress rely on the CRS for reports, studies, and answers to specific questions—information that helps them make good decisions.

The librarian of Congress is appointed by the president of the United States, and the Senate confirms the nomination. Among the important people who have held the post are Archibald MacLeish, a famous poet who succeeded Putnam in 1939, and a noted historian, Daniel Boorstin, who served from 1975 to 1987. The current librarian of Congress is Dr. James H. Billington.

Former librarians of Congress include poet Archibald MacLeish (above) and historian Daniel Boorstin (left).

THE THOMAS

The Thomas Jefferson Building is the most familiar of the three buildings that make up the Library of Congress. It is decorated with *paintings, stained glass, and statues* by many talented American artists.

JEFFERSON BUILDING

The Main Reading Room (below, left and right) is large enough for 250 readers to sit at individual desks. Its dome rises 160 feet (49 meters) above the floor. There are specialized rooms as well, which contain books about specific countries, cultures, and subjects. The Children's Literature Center has more than 180,000 books and other items, such as games and recordings.

More than Books

When you see the word "library," you think of books right away. But books are only a part of the material to be found in the Library of Congress. The manuscript collections include the journals, letters, and other private

Gordon Parks (center), is a photographer, writer, and composer, whose writings are part of the library's collection.

29

papers of presidents and other famous Americans. It also keeps original manuscripts of noted authors, such as Walt Whitman and Rudyard Kipling. Actual charts used by great explorers of the 1400s and 1500s are in the library's map and atlas collection, the largest in the world.

The library's permanent collection also includes more than 10 million graphic items such as prints, posters, cartoons, and photographs, as well as 100,000 motion pictures. It would take more than a lifetime to watch all the television programs and listen to all the recorded music and radio broadcasts carefully preserved in the Library of Congress.

Not every visitor to the library goes there for reading or research—or even to look at exhibits. Many attend concerts, movie screenings, lec-

tures, or poetry readings.
Every year, thousands of
music lovers enjoy the
library's classical music
concerts and outdoor folk
music performances.

A performance by the Juilliard
String Quartet

From the Gutenberg Bible to Books That Talk

Can any one book be singled out as the most treasured of the 27 million books in the Library of Congress? That honor belongs to the Gutenberg Bible. The Library of Congress has one of the three copies of the Bible that

Johannes Gutenberg and pages
from the Gutenberg Bible

still exist. It was printed by Johannes Gutenberg, who invented the printing press about 560 years ago. The Gutenberg Bible is one of the many permanent exhibits that make the Library of Congress an interesting museum as well as a library.

The library has a special division to serve the needs of those who are physically challenged. Blind people can choose from a vast collection of books and magazines in Braille, which is an alphabet made of small raised dots on paper that blind people can read with their fingers. Or they can listen to "talking books"— literary works read aloud on records or cassettes.

A book recorded on cassette (opposite page)

The Challenge of Time

Keeping the Library of Congress up-to-date is a big job. In a typical year, the library receives 9 million to 10 million new items and selects more than one million to go into the permanent collections.

The most serious challenge facing the library today is

Staff members receive millions of new items each year.

Books that have started
to fall apart

keeping books in good condition. Books are an "endangered species," in a sense—and it is not always the oldest books that are in the greatest danger. For about the last 150 years, most books have been printed on paper made from wood pulp. Over time, this paper falls apart. The Library of Congress has already put many books on microfilm, which is a system that stores books by

A Library of Congress employee works to preserve books.

photographing each page. It has also developed a process that chemically alters books to prevent decay. And it is now transferring books to discs that can hold 10,000 to 20,000 pages each.

The Library of Congress is racing against time to keep these priceless cultural resources from being lost forever. When you consider how many other problems have been solved by the librarians of Congress and their dedicated staffs, you can be confident that they will face this challenge successfully.

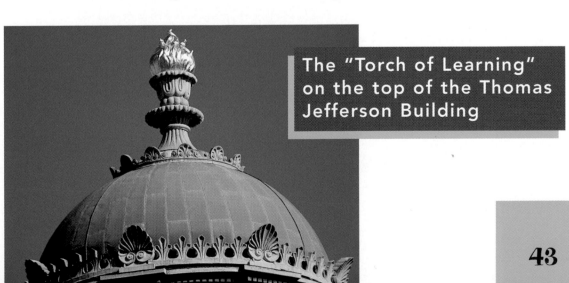

The "Torch of Learning" on the top of the Thomas Jefferson Building

To Find Out More

Here are some additional resources to help you learn more about libraries and the Library of Congress.

 **Books**

 **Organizations**

Fowler, Allan. **The Dewey Decimal System.** 1996. Children's Press.

Gibbons, Gail. **Check It Out! The Book About Libraries.** 1988. Harcourt and Brace.

Knowlton, Jack. **Books & Libraries**. 1991. Harper Collins Children's Books.

Santrey, Laurence. **Using the Library.** 1985. Troll Associations.

American Library Association
50 E. Huron St.
Chicago, IL 60611
312/ 440-9374
e-mail: *pio@ala.org*

Friends of Libraries U.S.A.
1700 Walnut Street
Philadelphia, PA 19103
(215) 790-1674

Library of Congress
Jefferson Building
1st Street, SE
Washington, D.C. 20540
e-mail: *lcweb@loc.gov*

Online Sites

Library of Congress Home Page

http.//www.loc.gov.

Information on the Library's collections and exhibits.

Library of Congress Online System (LOCIS)

http.//lcweb.loc.gov./home-page/online.html

The Library's collection of databases.

National Digital Learning Program

http://www.lcweb2.loc.gov./ammem/ndlpedu/index.html

A varied collection of online learning resources.

Events and Exhibits

http://lcweb.loc.gov./home-page/event.html

Learn about ongoing exhibits and upcoming events.

Historical Text Archive

http://www.msstate.edu/Archives/History

Explore historical documents, photographs, and diaries from many countries and time periods.

Important Words

acquire to gain something, either by having it given or by buying it

appoint to name someone to a position

bill the first draft of a law

database a large collection of information, usually in a computer

dome a large roof that looks like the top half of a ball

division a portion or section of a larger organization

endangered species a group (such as animals) that could die out if efforts are not made to save it

permanent lasting forever; a permanent collection stays at a museum all the time, while others might travel from place to place

spine the part of a book that faces out when the book is placed with others on a shelf; the spine usually lists the book title and the author's name

Index

Meet the Author

Allan Fowler is a freelance writer with a background in advertising. Born in New York, he now lives in Chicago and enjoys traveling.